Praise for **By Fire**

"Beautifully written and emotionally resonant."

- Literary Titan, Gold Award Winner

"Each piece in this collection is like a stained-glass scene of a Christian Midwestern family as seen through the eyes of a mature poet... In this poignant collection, Slota employs captivating imagery... A poetic, moving, and nuanced portrait."

- Kirkus Reviews

"A hauntingly beautiful collection... *By Fire* does justice to the life of those with mental illnesses and the effects it has on loved ones... [Slota] paints a life with so many brilliant colors that all fade at once before brightening up again."

- Independent Book Review

"Award-winning poet Rhonda Harris Slota has arrayed poignant, powerful childhood memories in this collection, with portraits of family that will burn in the reader's mind like the fire of the book's title."

- Feathered Quill

"To really know someone, you need to know their life story. Rhonda Harris Slota understands this truism... Rhonda writes as if she experienced this life. There are hints of joy as well as shadows of pain... Maturity allows us to see life in a new and different light. This collection is filled with emotion. I recommend this book as an insight into rural pastoral life."

- Readers' Favorite, 5-star review

By Fire

poems

Rhonda Harris Slota

atmosphere press

Published by Atmosphere Press

Cover design by Ronaldo Alves

Acrylic painting, "Pheonix Rising," by K.D. Self

Photograph by Reba Jewell Wiley

atmospherepress.com

CONTENTS

The following poems have previously appeared in print:

In *Cordella Magazine,* 2020
    "Dream"

In *Transfer Magazine,* 1991:
    "The Bottom Lands Are Flooded"
    "Prophet"
    "Annie"

In *The Napa Valley Review,*
Grand Prize Winner, American Poetry Association, 1983:
    "The Healer"

In *The Napa Valley Review, 1984*
    "Revelation"

In *En Vee Magazine:1992*
    "Only Twenty-Six"

In *The Bastard Review, 1991*
    "Pain"
    "Waiting for Salvation"

In *89 Cents, 1992*
    "A Rose Tatoo"

In *Artwell, 1991*
    "Mother"

In Remembrance:

Robert William Harris
1927 – 2018

Dianne Marie Aigaki
1947 – 2014

Janet Powell Yedes
1952 – 2019

"You must greet each day with a welcome heart,
for the sun must also rise in you
for the light to disperse the darkness."
Sri Anandamayi Ma

Someone I loved once gave me
a box full of darkness.
It took me years to understand
that this, too, was a gift.
-Mary Oliver
"The Uses of Sorrow"

THE BOTTOM LANDS
ARE FLOODED

Last night rain beat
the fields as if to pound
life from the ground.

Today, new plants
poke their heads
through a shining sheet of water.

My mother, in rubber boots,
hangs clothes on the line.
She smooths each shirt
with her hands as if it holds
someone she loves.

A fresh wind stirs the birches, wrinkles
a field of water. Mother frowns.
She hates the wind.

"Look," she says, "it unsettles
the trees. How lonely the world is."

THE HEALER

My father stands
behind the pulpit
lifting the Bible,
a black beacon,
high above his head.
He sees God gleam
in the grain of the beams.

His prayer for the girl
whose kidneys will fail her
tears through his body.
Power surges through his hands;
he holds her bowed head.

That night he kneels at the altar.
I go to him, place my palm on his shoulder.
He turns to me blood-rimmed eyes.

I remember my collie who leaped
into the road then turned
and saw the car.
I rushed to help; she snapped
her teeth, then lay still.
He pushes my hand away,
leaves the church.

Now, he says
his solitude saves him,
his fingernails stained
from factory work where he paints
the gashes in television cabinets.

He tells me the light hurts
his eyes. In dark glasses, he watches
his set: war death in Lebanon.
He whispers
"This is all prophesied;
the plan shaping itself around Persia."
His hands fold in his lap.

I am afraid to touch him.

JULY

beyond the oak trees

a rooster's ragged
edge of sound

hollow, desperate

a pear tree loaded
with young fruit

I lie down in
brown grass

the sky powders

a doe, two fawns rattle
dead thistles

nudging the earth
hopeful

a trickle of salty
liquid slides behind my ear

**

a hot day
my father and I
ride the sorrel mare

she runs us
under the pear tree

a low limb
knocks us off
breaks his
collarbone, gashes
my forehead

he heals,
gallops
the mare

through pastures,
orchards

powerful in his
discovery of her
nature, her need

my road splits apart
in jagged angles

I turn west
toward desert

**

my father wore
a prophet's skin

it does not
matter who gave
it to him

if he dies
before me
I want only

the thick
old Bible his
pale hands
cradled while

the lamp
glowed
beside him

the book he
held high
preaching
"oneness"

not unity
but one way

   **

I crave fire,
those strict words
he underlined

   **

this time of
year, no burning
allowed

the sun glares;
one glint could
catch broken
glass, ignite

   **

We have no church
to pray in

ANNIE AND ME

Silent edges, darkness,
breath inhaled deeply.

Annie, how can
you be locked
in a jail cell, your small
body immersed
in dark-eyed fear?

In this photo Mother
sent me, sorrow
ripens your face.

My love folds
you into my life.

We cannot return
to the days I placed
my hand over your eyes,
held you steady
with my breath.

I would take your pain
down, drown it in my
blood if I could.

GRANDMA'S KITCHEN TABLE

*

After platefuls of chicken,
dumplings, green beans
swimming in "seasoning,"
Grandma's name for bacon grease,
homemade fluffy biscuits and coconut pie,

when the women have finished all the cooking,
serving and cleaning up, the men retire,
full-bellied to the living room to talk
dirt-track racing, deer hunting
or simply drift off in a chorus of snoring.

*

The women sit down at Grandma's table.

She places a pot of hot coffee
in the center and gives us each a cup.
At ten, I am allowed to join them.
I can tolerate the bitter taste.

We drink coffee, eat pie, laugh,
or choke through tears
as the stories dip, drag, repeat
slide and dance for hours.

Story after story sutures secret
longings or painful memories,
weaving the weirdly funny
or tragic situations of living
poor in rural southern Indiana.

*

There are mysteries,
like Grandma's Cherokee
background which she hides
though it isn't clear why.
Grandma is generous, big-hearted, good-souled.
"You do me right, I'll give you the shirt off my back.
I'll cook my last morsel for you to eat.
But if you cross me, I cut you off!"

Despite quiet visits to North Carolina
relations, she never speaks their names.
Sometimes, we probe her with questions,
suspecting a Truth that might give us
another connection to the earth,
a missing thread of our history,
inherited wisdom that runs
deeply through our veins
like the slow crawl of creek water
along the rocks in late fall.
In winter, when the ice takes over,
We know the water is still underneath.

*

Sometimes, my aunts tell
stories they can only say
in the presence of each other.

My mother reveals
my first year of life.

"After my baby, Stephen, died,
I didn't think I could go on.
I was 17 years old, living in that two room
lean-to off the back of Mrs. Johnson's house
and your dad was already showing signs
of not being quite right in his mind."

All her sisters nod,
glance at me.
Suddenly, I feel embarrassed.

Mother looks into her black coffee
as though trying to read it like tea leaves,
then returns her eyes to mine.
"When I got pregnant again, I was sure it
would be a boy to replace the one I lost.

When you were born, I'm sorry now,
I just didn't want a girl. I tried to give
You away to the nurses at the hospital.
I only had a boy's name picked out."

Aunt Audrey leans toward me,
her voice edged
with melancholy, "I named you."
"I told your mommy,
'You have to give that child a name. Then,
You'll be able to love her.'"

I was given a name.
I wonder when my
Mother began to love me.

*

I learn that I spent my first months
in pain, screaming for nourishment.

"We thought you had the colic.
When your dad came home from work
I practically threw you at him.
I was miserable.

Then, one day, one of the church sisters
said to me, 'That baby is starving!'
She made a bottle of canned
Milnot and Karo syrup.
You drank it up and never had colic again.
I guess my milk wasn't any good.
From then on, that's what I fed my babies."

*

Years later at that same table,
a summer storm rattles the windows.
Outside, maples and poplars stand
their ground, challenging the wind
and bend almost to breaking.
Humidity and darkness seep into the room.

The two youngest of the seven siblings
have been gone awhile: cancer.
Grandpa has succumbed to a stroke.
I am almost forty.

Aunt Roberta laughs about the trip
she took in her twenties to the
Cumberlands to see where Johnnie
from the Carnival lived.
"She always had the wanderlust,"
muses Grandma. "Kind of like you!"
She pats my hand.

The whirl of the electric fan stops
as the electricity gives way.
A line down somewhere.

Aunt Shirley takes out her guitar.

Together, we all sing
Patsy Cline's version
of "Crazy."

MIGRAINE

One eye wrenches
from its socket. Any
movement wraps me
in pain, sin.

Medication sends me away.

Mother's back porch -
geraniums, begonias,
impatiens spill
from hanging baskets.

Robins peck, peck,
peck at clusters
of red dogwood berries.

Caves. Every year
someone drowns.

I crawl for hours; my
flashlight searching
as white eyeless
salamanders squirm
through the streambed.

In a large room
delicate fins slope
from the slow
movement of water.

Music to the touch.

Assuring myself
there is nothing to fear
I shut off my light, enter
the infamous dark.

15

ONLY TWENTY-SIX

Mother bursts out from the
Southside Market, lets the door
bang behind her, gets in the car,
slams the bag down on the seat.

"What happened?" Dad asks, not
in his powerful preacher's voice,
but in the querulous tone of
a mildly irritated husband.

"When I took the bacon package
off the rack, some man whispered
to his Jezebel girlfriend, *Look
at that woman's dishpan hands*!"

My mother's hands are rough
from plunging her arms elbow-deep
in the ringer washer tub.
She swirls
the water in wide
hard circles, pulls with
all her weight, the shirts,
flattening, between the rollers.

"He's right, and I'm only twenty-six."

Dad gives the comfort he can, says
maybe she should try another
brand of soap. She is sobbing.
"You just don't know how
it is; I wish I were a man!"

In the car's back seat, I
shift uneasily, needing
reassurance, stand up, lean
forward between them: "Kids
have the best lives, don't they?"

Mother whirls around so fast
I fall backward. "But you will
grow up; then the fun's over, just wait."

Eighteen years later, my twenty-sixth
birthday, I wake up early.

As my husband sleeps, I creep
from the bed to our
kitchen, sit down at the table,
look hard at my hands.

PROTECTION

On hot sticky
mid-western nights
Annie and I listen

to the "plink, plink"
of jar lids sealing
until we sleep.

Mother stays awake
all night counting.

The next morning
she searches for
the ones that haven't
sealed. She knows
exactly how many.

For days the kitchen steams,
covered with the dust
and cement smell
of lime and the stronger
sweet smell of cloves.

Annie and I,
stuffed with pickles,
run out
into the muggy
sunlight.

We stretch out
on the hammock
slung between
two poplars.

She lays her hand
on my arm, presses until
it annoys me
and I move.

She grins, then
I know she is
pestering.

I always feel guilty
about Annie, so I protect
her. There was that one

time when I sang soprano
in the school choir. I
was sixth grade, Annie
second. I fainted.

Dead away as Mother
would say. I don't know
why. The heat was too high
or my clothes were too heavy.

I watched Mr. Wilson's baton
moving, directing, and
moving and moving,

and then, the janitor
was carrying me out of
the dizzying darkness.

In the nurse's room, a cold
cloth on my head, I heard
a worried second grade
teacher say "May her
sister see her?"

Poor Annie. She
thought I had died
in the middle
of "Silent Night."

I clung to her
soft weeping body,
promised never
to be weak again.

REVELATION

The child wakes up to hymns
sung by her father. His hands clap,
jubilant, echo from the hall.
She tiptoes to her bedroom door,
opens it enough to see him
standing in dim light praising
God for the gift of prophesy,
while the mother holds on
to the wall. The child
is not afraid.

She remembers rituals
unannounced. He rampages, purging
the house. From every room he
snatches the false things, flings
open the front door and throws
out red plastic flowers, a can
of hair spray, a fashion magazine.
Entering the yard,
he rips the dental plate
from his own mouth.

The mother cringes, hurries
after him, gathering
photographs, the radio, his teeth.
She trudges back to the house,
closes the door. Suddenly alone, he
stops, lowers his head, cries.
The child watches from the window.

Ambulance doors lock behind
him. The mother tells her sister,
"It's like sending him to prison."
But she must do it. He frightens
her. She is tired. The child
who has been sent to her room
crouches behind the couch, wants
to touch her mother's arm, still
hears her father's song.

He returns. The child searches
his face as he speaks, glances
toward the door. He tells her
he has witnessed Truth, wants
to share the sight of vision
born of flame. But sanity
means following the rules.

He has opened his arms
to lightning.

The child shivers.
Is her father's
life her own?

*Children, until they say 'I' or 'me' or their name, are rooted
in the collective unconsciousness.*
          C.G. Jung, Eunice Jung and Tom Wolff,
          <u>A Collection of Remembrances</u>

OCTOBER

More than usual, October
is the time of year
my mother cries.

The days are too
orange-red-beautiful.
They hurt.
The way the light
gradually softens,
the wind won't quit.

Brittle maple leaves
scrape across the roof,
slip to the ground.
She sweeps them into piles
the wind picks up
in quick gusts.

She never gives up.
She weeps
and burns piles
of leaves every day.
Thick smoke rises
through the trees.

She wants to protect
every blade of summer grass
until it turns brown.

Then, she stands at the back door
looking out across the fading,
as if there is something more
she could have done.

DREAM

It glides slowly
its barrel-like body,
brown and white markings, massive
pipe-lengths slumbering
over the sofa, languidly
surrounding a table.

I am situated uneasily
in this room, hot, humid
summer afternoon.

My father lives here; it is
our home, but different.

His hair is darker, eyes
sunken into their depths.

The heavy undulating
mass appears now
and then over and under
the furniture, in
and out of rooms.

I say to my father, "Please
get it out of here
before dark.
I want to sleep. How can I
knowing it is here but not
where it is?"

A stranger, wearing a
white gown, appears at the door.
He pulls from behind him
a chattering rattler, throws it.

My head snaps around
as a huge python mouth erupts
from behind the couch, grabs
the sizzling smaller reptile, spitting
red and yellow fire.

*

I think of the closet
I hid in as a child,
its cool darkness one kind
of fear, another the sudden
glare of light should someone
open the door, flip the switch,
expose my small self.

I do not understand
from where salvation
comes. I am weighted
by the tonnage of mystery.

Oblivious, then too much
aware of the insidious,
the stunning crackle,
a sudden silence.

My father and I
are not safe in
any house.

WAITING FOR SALVATION

His enemies would cut
off my hands and feet.
I hid because he
said I should.

Isn't he to be pitied,
who taught me
life is a dark closet,
the smell of mothballs, soft
sleeves of old coats?

When the furnace came
on, the wood floor shuddered,
shrank. I was thrilled by the
unknown light hovering
at the fringes of darkness.

Stephen, my dead brother,
sat down beside me, held
my frozen hands.
I was saved.

Hidden now by the shadows
of miles, still hearing my father's
fierce declarations of faith,
his charge that outsiders
would destroy his flesh –

How readily
I would have given
my limbs
to save him.

PROPHET

Elijah, the Prophet, dumps his life
in a sack, throws it over his shoulder,
heads for the cave.
There, he lifts his eyes and cries, "Where
is the chariot, my promised
horses of flame?

I have heard your still voice; angels
have gathered me in their wings.
What good can my weakness do you?"

He is lifted; the ground turns to ashes.

1

My father searches for salvation
in God's power. Stained windows
glare. Dogma smothers his faith.

The congregation shouts,
reels in a spell, the Holy Ghost.

He remembers his mother forcing
him to touch his dead grandfather.
After that, even the softness of living
flesh given to his hands terrifies him.

2

Deacons squint; tight suits
pinch their bodies.
Long-sleeved dresses,
cotton stockings cover
the pale-skinned women,
their hair piled in great hives.

They murmur of Sin, their backsliding
Brother. A mob of whisperers
preys upon him.

3

Wilderness emerges from his eyes
when the Bible he holds begins to tremble.
His body aches from the weight of the past:
his mother's thick hands shaping biscuits,
the blaze in her eyes,
reflection of the fire ring
he set in the neighbor's field
while he stood in the center
wondering if he could
smother it in time.

4

When our bravery sags,
Solitude becomes our refuge.
Father, before
you return to the cave,
Listen. Remember the Voice
you once described as Stillness
so loud it roars.
Can you hear it?

5

His voice hollows, an ancient poverty
reaches out from inside and pulls
the tongue back, the breast-bone opens
exposing vessels of sacred fluid.

Was he deluded,
did some nail pluck, pluck
away at the nerves?

6

Who assigned him
this Righteousness
he cannot endure?
He taught me to beware
the worldly ones,
but the world will not fade,
even a little, because of us.

An apple in his hand darkens
as it does in mine.
We expect nothing
of the other now, each of us
alone and the same

since that first night
I woke up, heard him
singing and clapping
his hands in the hallway
outside my door.

TO BE SAVED

Stephen, my older

brother, the first son
my mother worshipped
died too soon.

Death
predicted by a wild
bird loose in the house.

The omens
in our lives are
clear, indisputable.

Circles

my mother's dark
eyes. The slough

at the foot of the hill
rimmed with cattails

the water ripples
when a stone enters

everything remains
the same, yet changes

with every breath.

Tent Revival

Rows of folding chairs
on the parched field grass.

Yellow bulbs hang
around the seam like
over-sized Christmas lights.

A fine mist of dust.

Every night for a week,
we clap our hands and sing
"At the cross, where I
first saw the light."

My body tingles;
the familiar words roll
off my tongue.

When they take
to the aisles, the pain

in my throat is my own
voice tearing loose.

No one hears me.

      Aunt Audrey, beautiful,
      refined, dances barefoot.

      Her path, like her life,
      clearly defined, solidly set
      on the straight and narrow.

She holds her arms in right
angles, an Egyptian dancer,
upper arms parallel
to the ground, fingertips
lifted toward the tent top,
her black hair streaming.

When my mother "shouts,"
her eyes roll upward, her
head falls back as though severed.

The handkerchief she holds
by one corner, flutters
like dove feathers, in
front of her, behind her.

What does her heart feel,
her mind know, eyes
lifted, nothing but whites,
to the point of disappearing?

       My mother leaves me. She
       whirls like a dervish.

       I beg God
       to let her live.

His Dance

Behind the pulpit
in baggy suit, narrow
tie, my father's dance is slow,
controlled. Ironically smiling
he claps his hands

confined to his own
circle of light.

He is the prophet
Elijah whose prayers
are answered
by fire.

He is
Flame

straining upward.

Hidden

In Mother's dresser
drawer, a picture
of the child, Stephen,
in his casket,
dried white carnations.

When she thinks
I am napping, she goes to
the drawer, opens it
takes out the picture,
hugs it to her breast.

Baptism

The deacons lead me,
robed, barefoot, down
the cold steps into the cement
baptismal's blue water.

On the limestone wall,
a painting of bearded men
in flowing white, worshiping
beside the River Jordan.

Replicas of palm trees
I have never seen
hover above me.

Singing and clapping
their hands with joy
just for me, those
familiar faces gleam.

Debbie is there; she once
held my hand in a sink
of scalding water, repented,
left me with the scar
of not forgetting.

And Leah whose sense
of destiny is sharper
than mine reminds
me of my spiritual lack,
warns of the choice:
baptism or fire.

My mother is afraid of water.
I search their faces
for hers. Cannot find it.

There He stands,
triumphant, proud.

The deacon, waist-deep,
turns me around
to face the front
of the tank. He shows me
how to hold my hands
over my nose, my
shoulders barely above water.
He places one large hand
over my cupped hands,
another at my back.

Bowing his head
he prays. "I baptize
you in the name of Jesus Christ."

He thrusts me backward –
the water and panic gather
like wings; I am lifted.

Emerging, I reach
my hands far up,
crying with gratitude,
as so many before me,
water pouring down around me.

I see their glowing faces,
hear singing,
the clapping hands.

Now,
I am sure
to be saved.

Holy Ghost

"The Kingdom of God is within you." (Luke 17:21)

I cannot conjure those
other tongues to speak
through my mouth.

I kneel at the altar
while saved Brothers
and Sisters send their pleading
cries upward, hold my hands
toward the rafters
until my arms go numb.

Tired of calling, "Jesus,"
my mouth loses its shape.

Aching, I open my eyes
wondering what the
others feel.

★

One day,
I learn
from a Yogi

to find the
Kingdom
within

by Being

Still.

Elijah

I dislike my grandma telling
me I look like great grandpa
Elijah until I see his picture.

His dark eyes, serious, maybe kind,
no ancient disapproving glare,
less dreadful than my father's memory.

Elijah died young, before
I was born, plowing
his field for corn.

Payne Cemetery on the hillside
among the oaks, sycamores, pines –
Elijah's stone, larger
than Stephen's, tilts
the same way.

Failure

He persuades doctors
to let him haul
a porcelain tub into
Aunt Linda's hospital room.

> He says baptism
> in one name,
> and the gift
> of Holy Ghost, our
> only salvation.

All night,
he paces, clasping,
unclasping his hands,
whispering, "Lord, let her live."

Early morning, she fights
from the darkness, asks for water,
drinks deeply, falls back.

She passes without
speaking in other tongues,
the gift denied.

> Over fields deep
> with snow, a crow calls
> from the elm.

> White powder
> falls - a branch
> suddenly naked.

PAIN

Father's head needs
real, physical pressure.

He wears Mother's iron
skillet like a hat.

Amber burning in Father's
eyes, he whispers,

"chartreuse," cannot
escape those chartreuse
eyes.

BATS

One night I sit in the
front seat of my father's
car while he goes inside
an unfamiliar house.

Among the crickets
in the summer air
I hear the lilting
strain – a woman's laugh
steps through the night.

> Above the porch
> light, a brown form
> seems to fold
> into itself
> against the eaves.
>
> *Bats flash down,*
> *entangle their feet*
> *in your hair. You*
> *have no choice*
> *but to burn them out.*

"Who is she?" I ask
my father, then
my brother. "An angel,"
says my father. "She is a
witch," says my brother.

My mother's eyes
seek the floor; "Thief,"
she whispers. "Help
me." I follow
her to the kitchen.

Outside the window,
pink faces grin,
black wings flap upward
into moonlight.

JADE

Mother outlines
her eyes with black
pencil, puts on
lipstick.

She loves a man not
her husband, touches
his tan skin, smoothes
the imprint where
a scar creases his cheek.

Beside White River, far down
in the reeds, she finds
a green stone - its color flashing
in sunlight. She thinks
it precious, like jade,

the name
she will give their son.

TOMORROW, I GO TO INDIANA FOR CHRISTMAS

today I talk
to my mother
an hour
long distance

what more
to say

what changes in
light of vision

*

My friend, Leonore,
stops by with her
children - we pick

lemons from the tree,
slice, eat them

tear stale bread,
throw it to
goldfish in the pond

frogs - green, orange
ones, wide-eyed,
Ernie tells me
pulling my sleeve, see?

*

at Indianapolis
airport, my mother
will enfold me

beyond her shoulder,
my nephew's ten-year-old,
hard-won grin

waits for me
to hold him.

I will look at the niece
I know from photographs,
wide laugh,
pink gums –

her father, seventeen,
my brother, Jade, holds
her like a
big round toy.

Mother, the tender
auburn-haired woman
who gives away
her strength,

will trudge across
the hard-packed snow,
climb into the car
beside me

a thin line
of sadness
showing

she counts
the days
until
I leave.

THE WOMAN IN A RED SEQUINED HAT

Some trust only pain.

> On the plane, I am seated
> two rows behind her.
>
> She bends forward, places
> a white vinyl bag under
> the seat. Magenta sparks fly
> against the wall, the small window.
>
> I remember my dream: sparks
> spitting from the python's
> mouth as it eats
> up a rattler.

My father's religion says
that hat is too loud, calls
attention to the woman.

> When I fell from
> the swing set, fractured
> my leg, pain transformed
> to bits of dancing color.
>
> My father carried me
> to the doctor. I was safe.

He is not one for snake
handling like some he knows -
that is occult,
a deliberate test of faith.

Elijah prayed for heavenly fire
in a contest: His God
against the heathen, Baal.

In church we sing – "Elijah prayed
and the fire came down."

> One day I pick up
> a jagged rock, slam it,
> again and again into my hand,
> run to my father.
>
> He takes from his pocket
> the white handkerchief
> he waves in the air
> when he preaches hell-fire,
> wraps it gently
> around my bleeding hand.

BURNING LEAVES

Burnt leaves whirl,
                    Crazy
            Tomorrow, more
                        Rustlers
Coloring the limbs
                    Will drop
That robin's
                    Nest has clung
            For years
                    She could climb the
Ladder
            Shake them all
                    Down
                            For the fire

                    Or she could fall
If reason
            Lost her

VISITING GRANDPA'S STORIES

55

That sawmill took
The life out of me, or
Them seven kids,
I don't know which.

Maybe it was buryin'
Two of them.
No parent should
Have to do that.

Never thought I'd see
The day when my kids had
To give me money to buy
Bacon and eggs.

Social security, that's
A joke, hon,
There ain't no security
In this life.

You're the smart one.
Put yourself
Through college.
Got out of here.

I only finished third grade.
Had to work after
Dad died and left
Us eleven kids with Mom.

I'm not ashamed
Of how hard I worked.
But I don't like
Limpin' around.

Look at these busted-up
Hands. This finger
Sticks straight out,
Won't move.

The other day,
Some guy got mad,
Thought I was makin'
An obscene gesture.

Why do you come back
Here anyway, and sit
Listenin' to an old man,
Talk about nothin'

Goddamnit,
Are you cryin'?

DISPLACED IN TIME

(For my maternal grandfather's sister)

Earl's rough hands
Grasp the saw handles

Blades scream
Through timber

Sawdust spewing

*

Darvill clasps a
Handful of violets

Against her white
Cotton dress

The day
They marry

*

The big lumber
Company moves in

With fancy equipment
Younger hands

*

Earl, the new
Night watchman

Darvill raises
African Violets

They grow
Older, Childless,

Laid off from the
factory, Earl tries farming

*

Cold winters
Cutting wood

Each morning
The house fills

With smells of
Coffee, biscuits

Bacon sizzling

*

This morning, a full
Kettle on the stove

Cold dishwater
In the sink.

Darvill, dead on her
Braided rug

Out between the rows
Of corn lies Earl

The gun still
in his hand

ANNIE

She trudges Ramada Inn hallways in her brown
polyester uniform and thick-soled shoes,
shakes blue cleanser on porcelain
fixtures and lets it set while she
yanks wrinkled sheets
from double beds impressed
with burdens of strangers.
She has seven hours to scrub
seventeen rooms to perfection.
They don't let her work full-time.

Caught in a whip of wind,
leaves skim the parking lot.
She races to her blue Camaro and lights
a cigarette, fights the gear-shift
knob for power and rumbles
off toward the day care center.

She stiffens with each
of her daughter's raw coughs,
fastens plastic around
the trailer windows, slices
potatoes, pats rounds
of hamburger into her mother's
iron skillet.

Grey clouds pick
up speed as the wind
blows in from the west.

A ROSE TATTOO

Mother and I,
stark figures
in emergency
room light,
looking down
at Annie.
Annie's breast,
reveals a rose
tattoo.

Mother reaches down,
pulls up the sheet.

The nurse
holds a paper bag
over Annie's mouth,
speaks in soft monotone.

Treatment
for hyperventilation
is simple: trap
the body's own
carbon-dioxide,
force it back
into the lungs.

All I see
of Annie
are eyes
traced
in thick liner,
long fingers
as calloused as Mother's
from scrubbing
other people's
floors.

The rose creeps out.
Etched in flesh,
it throbs
with quickened breath.
The pattern of miniscule
skin pricks blooms.

Under the sheet,
a wilderness pants,
demands freedom.

When
her breath
retreats to normal,
I carry Annie
across the frozen
parking lot.

In our haste
we forgot to bring
her shoes.

The pneumonia
inside her
thin body
rattles
against me.

Mother sobs,
"Annie,
how could you?"

TORNADO

*

On a stormy summer day
my mother remembers
she once felt beautiful
while five miles away,
my nineteen-year-old brother
drives through the torrential
in his '65 Ford pick-up.

*

Jade, bursts through the door!
"Man, you won't believe
what happened.
You almost lost me!
Sorry, Mom,
I may need a new truck!"

Mother gives him her seat,
places a steaming cup
in front of him,
her hand on his shoulder.

Jade looks up.
Light dancing
in dark deep-set eyes.

"I learned one thing,
Don't ever try
to outrun a tornado!"

He tells the story.

Before the funnel's
tail takes the truck,
he kicks open the door, leaps
into a ditch, while wind, rain
and debris whirl around him.
Six feet away, a lightning bolt
slams the trembling ground.

*

We relish his presence,
the raw humor, his ruddy
skin, black curly hair,
his swagger
when he enters a room.

He who sobs when his best
dog friend, Pancho, dies.
Walks deep
into the woods with a shovel.
Sits till dawn watching
the little grave,
listening
to distant coyotes
yip through the night.

A worthy successor to
the son she lost
long ago.

The fear
of what did not happen
this time
unwinds,

dissolves
like vapor
in the heavy air.

63

TO MYSELF: THE CHILD
WHO HID IN CLOSETS

I welcome you to sunlight,
to walk the path
through green trees
toward the dark pond
nestled in a tangle of
leaves and moss where
you ran until your
Mother's shrill voice
called you back.

I forgive you for the times
you kept running,
splashed through
the mucky water, found
your favorite poplar and
hoisted yourself up
branch by branch
until the wind
made you pause,

forcing her to cut a switch
and wait for you on the back
porch step. She hated
to do it, but you
needed to learn.

*

I forgive you
for the time,
you chose
a fistful of pills,
the best path to peace
you could find.

What could have been more
untenable than hiding
in a dark closet calling
forth a ghost to take your hand
or grasping the top
branches of a Poplar
dreading to come down
and face the stinging sassafras,
and worse, your father's frantic eyes?

And where did you get sleeping pills?

I remember looking down
at you, barely a teenager.
When you awoke, anger
flashed in your eyes,
your skin pallid, hair
damp and matted,
knowing they would ask, though
you knew no answer to say aloud,
"Why don't you know you are loved?"

*

My journey has led me to
countless angels
who will not let me die.
I want to take you
to the path, lit by the full-moon,
Mother of mothers, who manages
the rhythms of the seas.

Find your feet, let the tap root
run down through your soles
deep into the ground.
Find your hands, let the pulse
give them strength to carry
and tenderness to touch.

Your heart needs time
to know what it feels.

Remember your Self
with kindness, feel
the peace, the joy
that settles beyond
the needs of each day.

I want to tell you,

Love is neither
want nor need;
it is freedom from both,
the Bliss that awakens,

enfolds us as we
reach Inward
or out to another.

It is a quiet voice
that powerfully
whispers,

"Live!"

APOLOGIES

He laughs
nervously through
the crackle of phone
wires frozen over
deep snow, the peppery
tracks of birds.

"I don't know
what gets into me.
Everything
and nothing
makes sense

all at once. I don't
want to hear the
past drug up. Why
can't we let
things rest?"

He means this,
his apology, the closest
I will get to affection.

*

Christmas night
in his trailer
drinking cheap champagne
we argued about
religion.

He told me I was
his most difficult
child, the one who
challenged, questioned,
the one he least
understood.

I slammed his door,
a half-empty
bottle in my hand,
trudged the icy road
back to my mother's house.
Let's do forget.
Then, I hear
my voice saying
I'm not ready.

I waited him out,
I think, a burst of pride,
then shame, knowing
I would have searched

until I found him, alone
on the bench where
he rests under the
frosted trees

or strolling the gilded
Mall corridor
walking his daily
routine since the heart
operation, retirement.

I would have sought him
because there is a
wrongness in our anger;
it clunks
like the sour ivory
on Grandmother's
old upright piano.

My father is
telling me he
is sorry without
saying so and I
do the same. Tomorrow,
we will meet and walk
through the Mall together.

Is it really over, the
waiting in closets
for the Holy Ghost

to appear, fearing
the preacher's righteous
bellow, trying to rid
myself of sins committed
too long ago to believe?

MY FATHER AND I BY FIRE

Under an expanse of stars
his eyes lock on the dark
distance of fir trees or some
ancient thought he half remembers
but can't place, like remnants
of a troubling dream at dawn.

I toss a log on the campfire;
little splinters of flame hit
the air, light his face. He sits
whittling, with no sign
of conviction, at a hunk of wood.

Tonight he is calm. What doctors call
hallucination is vision to him.
Smiles are abhorrent to one
whose instincts detect hypocrisy.

It was long ago that
his terror happened.

Then, his hands frightened
him when cold air plunged
down his arms, turned to fire
as it rushed out the fingers.

He remembers the day
he entered the state hospital,
how the patients stood
in recognition when
they saw him there –
nothing more to lose.

LETTING GO

(February, 2018)

He did not allow
his children to hug him
so we found other ways
to feel his touch; me by
hurting myself, to be carried
to a doctor or bandaged by his hands.
He only placed his palms
on other heads bowed in prayer.

Though he never said so,
we know he loved us.

On the final day of his life,
I sit by his bedside and read
John 3:17, wanting
the last words
he hears to be that
Jesus came to sow Love,
not to condemn.

His bird-thin fingers claw
at the air, his
nearly sightless eyes
focus on mine.
"Am I alive?
Yes, Dad, and I'm here.
"Oh, I thought I was dead."

He falls back, mouth open.
That labored breathing again.
His hand drops to the page.

"Dad, your palm
is resting
on Psalms 93," I
tell him though I don't know
if he hears me. I read,
The Lord is robed in majesty,
and armed with strength.

Do I imagine
the smile flickering
on his pale thin lips?

He takes no more food. No water.

Yesterday, his reed–like fingers,
dark–veined, grasped
red grapes on his tray
placing them like rare
delicacies between pursed lips,
rolling them side to side
in his mouth, savoring.

*

Now, we clasp his hands,
pat skin covering bone,
tell him through tears, "We love
You, Dad. It's OK to go."

Suddenly, his eyes open,
his mouth attempts
to form words.

We each interpret
what he tried to say
according to the
comfort we need.
Did he say" See you later,"
"I love you," or was he
greeting God?

I watch his eyes soften
to that distance beyond
human sight, his hard
breath stutters, then stills.

His passing does not
leave a wound,
but a softness, a vast
unyielding silence, a lifting.

I see his spirit flutter, a moth
with orange and gold wings
like delicate flames
at the light, a faint shadow
casting off for freedom.

I walk away at peace.
I have witnessed
a remarkable,
a terrible beauty,
the end of my
father's earthly life.

MOTHER

Under a perfect summer sky, corn
    shrivels in the fields

Still she fills her shelves with jars of tomatoes, green beans,
    Plenty to share with the neighbors, she says

She opens to me her hands
    hardened from heaving buckets of water

Shakes her head – the weeds
    outlive her efforts to defeat them

Showing me how the vine shrinks
    as the young squash grow larger

Leaves brushing her ankles
    she leans on her hoe

She is wise as the farmer feeling the ache of rain
    seep through the bones before it comes

I rub the bump of skin on my chin
    appearing in the same place as hers
    her lines deepen around my mouth

I notice I'm taller than her – just barely
    wondering what things she
    has not yet told me

She gives water to the parched earth

ACKNOWLEDGEMENTS

Paula Amen-Judah, exquisite writer, meticulous editor, and fiercely supportive friend without whose encouragement and skills this book would not have come to fruition. There are not enough words to fully express my gratitude.

Frances Mayes and William S. Dickey, my mentors at San Francisco State University, whose wisdom and professional expertise helped me find more precision, clarity and focus in my work.

Janet Powell Yedes, intelligent, insightful, loving fellow Hoosier and traveler in this lifetime. The last night we were together before her illness and passing, we stayed up until 3:00 am while I read her these poems. Many of her smallest changes made profound differences in their quality and depth. The impact of her love and friendship knows no bounds.

Dianne Aigaki, who continuously encouraged with her open-hearted love, unbridled courage and world-wide wisdom. She inspired and encouraged me through every obstacle. Her presence lives in these pages and in my heart.

Napa Valley Poetry Group including Dave Evans, Warren Bean, Leonore Wilson, Richard Slota, Maggie Tuteur.
We met in the 80's, and the writing process began in earnest for me. We labored over many of the poems in this book and I feel their presence throughout.

Maggie Tuteur, sister-friend, her intriguing stories and stunning poems, her connectedness with the natural world and its teachings continue to inspire and bless.

Thomas Avena, exquisite poet, AIDS activist, and generous friend, the first to publish some of these poems in his magazines. He shared his stage with me on a reading tour in San Francisco.

K. D. Self, for her editing, her laughter, her love, and her strength, whose powerful artwork, compassion and heart inspired the cover.

Deni Hodges, skilled editor, devoted friend and Gabriel's dear Auntie, whose spirit brings light and changes the world daily.

Atmosphere Press for publishing this 30 + years labor of love. I deeply appreciate the effective, efficient, and positive support at all levels. Thank you, Nick Courtright, Trista Edwards, Erin Larson, Ronaldo Alves and Evan Courtright for your guidance, wisdom, professionalism and heart throughout the publishing process.

Rajashree Maa for her limitless love, Marilyn Knight-Mendelson for the years of daily heart-full sharing, Dariece Warren (mid-western buddy, sister Yogini), Daphne Birkmyer (family, friend, confidante, excellent writer), Sandra Lee (sister devotee and Yogini), Barbara Schwartz (fearless technical wizard, designer, friend), Carolynne Gamble (brilliant artist, designer, friend), Dinndayal Morgan (spiritual brother), and so many more angels/poets/friends who have influenced these poems and touched my life.

My family who has lived through so many triumphs and tragedies with courage, integrity and love.

My Aunt Roberta Mann who encouraged me in my early twenties to dream big, attend University, to travel and to write.

My son, Gabriel, who teaches me daily about unconditional love, compassion and acceptance.

My beloved Guru, Paramahansa Yogananda, for everything.

ABOUT
ATMOSPHERE PRESS

Atmosphere Press is an independent, full-service publisher for excellent books in all genres and for all audiences. Learn more about what we do at atmospherepress.com.

We encourage you to check out some of Atmosphere's latest releases, which are available at Amazon.com and via order from your local bookstore:

Damaged, poetry by Crystal Wells

I Would Tell You a Secret, poetry by Hayden Dansky

Aegis of Waves, poetry by Elder Gideon

Footnotes for a New Universe, by Richard A. Jones

Streetscapes, poetry by Martin Jon Porter

Feast, poetry by Alexandra Antonopoulos

River, Run! poetry by Caitlin Jackson

Poems for the Asylum, poetry by Daniel J. Lutz

Licorice, poetry by Liz Bruno

Etching the Ghost, poetry by Cathleen Cohen

Spindrift, poetry by Laurence W. Thomas

A Glorious Poetic Rage, poetry by Elmo Shade

Numbered Like the Psalms, poetry by Catharine Phillips

Verses of Drought, poetry by Gregory Broadbent

Canine in the Promised Land, poetry by Philip J. Kowalski

PushBack, poetry by Richard L. Rose

Modern Constellations, poetry by Kendall Nichols

ABOUT THE AUTHOR

Rhonda Harris Slota grew up in Bloomington, Indiana and received her BA in English from Indiana University. She moved to northern California in 1982. She was awarded the Jessamyn West Creative Writing Poetry Award from Napa Valley College in both 1983 and 1984 and received the Grand Prize from the American Poetry Association in 1983. She completed her MA in English/Creative Writing at San Francisco State University in 1991. Her career pathway led to teaching and administration in secondary, community college and adult education. She retired in 2016 as Napa Valley Adult Education Principal after 30 + years in public education. She lives in Vallejo, California with her son, continues to write poetry, teaches Yoga and consults as a Certified Ayurvedic Practitioner, Ayurvedic Yoga Therapist, and Kali Ki Reiki Master and Teacher. Visit Rhonda at www.ByFirePoetry.com or at www.TheJourneyToWellness.com.

www.ingramcontent.com/pod-product-compliance
Lightning Source LLC
Chambersburg PA
CBHW011936050726
47590CB00011B/3324